Calligraphy Book for Beginners

_____

_____

© 2024 QuillScribe Memoirs

All rights reserved. No part of this publication may be reproduced, distributed, or transmitted in any form or by any means, including photocopying, recording, or any other electronic or mechanical methods, without the prior written permission of the author or publisher.

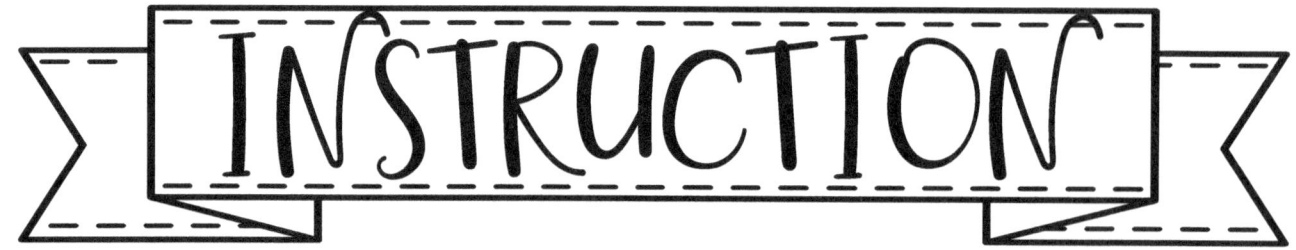

Fundamentals of Lettering

Mastering the art of lettering starts with a few basics. Good posture and pen grip may seem simple but are crucial for your progress.

Sitting Right

Consider your posture as the foundation of lettering. Sit where your feet are firmly on the ground, and you have enough space to move your arm freely. This position allows for better control. Use your other hand to keep the paper still for more precision.

Pen Mastery

When you grip your pen, aim for a balance – not too tight, not too loose. The angle of your pen is key to producing beautiful strokes. Don't worry if it's not perfect at first. Think of it as learning to walk; it takes time and persistence. Keep practicing, and you'll see your skills grow.

Essential Lettering Tools

If you're excited about starting lettering, you might want to buy all sorts of tools, but you really don't have to spend a lot. For our purposes, we'll stick to the basics: a Fudenosuke Pen and a Brush Pen. But here are some other tools you might consider:

Pencils: They're easy to find and good for beginners.

Pens: Start with any pen you have. Micron pens are nice, but even a gel pen or felt tip works.

Brush Pens: They're like fancy quill pens but be careful, they can be addictive and tricky to use at first.

Watercolors: Fun for creating with colors, you can use different brushes for different effects.

Chalk: You can find special markers to create chalk designs that look stunning.

Paper: The book has space for practice, but for more practice, get some thick card stock paper. It's better than regular thin paper.

Fudenosuke Pen: We're using this fine-tipped pen in the book for neat, single-line writing. You can buy it at any craft store.

Brush Pen: Great for when you want to try more elaborate calligraphy and designs.

Learning Strokes

This style is sometimes called "easy calligraphy" because it's straightforward and quick. It's all about making lines look even and smooth – like drawing with one of those cool pens you see on craft sites. You move your pen just like in the Brush Alphabet, but keep the pressure the same all the time. No need for heavy lines here! You can even use normal pens, but a smaller tip is better.

1  2  3  4

5  6  7  8

Strokes:

1 Light lines going up.

2 Heavy lines going down.

3 Curves starting from the bottom going up.

4 Curves starting from the top going down.

5 Loops reaching high.

6 Loops going low.

7 Shapes like an egg.

8 Fancy S-like shapes.

Upstrokes

Start from the bottom and go up.

Keep the line thin.

Don't press too hard.

Downstrokes

Start from the top and go down.

Press harder for a thicker line.

Start with less pressure, press more as you go down, then let up at the end.

Underturn Stroke

Start with a thick line going down.

Then make a thin line going up.

Overturn Stroke

Start with a thin line going up.

Then make a thick line going down.

Ascending Loop

Make a thin line that curves up and over.

Descending Loop

Make a thin line that curves down and under.

Oval

Make a looped shape like a sideways egg.

Compound Curve

Start with a curve up then a bigger curve down, like a wave.

Your practice is a serene garden where skills blossom quietly but surely. It's not just about the perfection of each letter, but the joy and peace you find with each motion. Celebrate the small victories, the first time your loop closes just right, the moment your strokes start to flow together in harmony.

You hold more than just a pen; you hold a magic wand that transforms simple words into art. The paper is your canvas, and every word you write is a brushstroke of your soul. Be gentle with yourself, and let the positivity in your heart guide your hand. The beauty of your journey lies in the journey itself, not just the destination.

With each new page, you turn over, approach it with a smile. For in this craft, every moment is a step forward, a reason to be proud. So take a deep breath, and let your creativity soar. The world of calligraphy is brighter with you in it.

Take this message to heart and let the positivity fuel your practice sessions.

Happy writing!

UPERCASE LETTERS
trace and repeat

A

UPERCASE LETTERS
trace and repeat

B

UPERCASE LETTERS
trace and repeat

C

UPERCASE LETTERS
trace and repeat

V

UPERCASE LETTERS
trace and repeat

E E E E E E

UPERCASE LETTERS
trace and repeat

J

UPERCASE LETTERS
trace and repeat

G

UPERCASE LETTERS
trace and repeat

H H H H H

H H H H H

H H H H H

H H H H H

H H H H H

UPERCASE LETTERS
trace and repeat

J

UPERCASE LETTERS
trace and repeat

J

UPERCASE LETTERS
trace and repeat

K

UPERCASE LETTERS
trace and repeat

L

UPERCASE LETTERS
trace and repeat

M

UPERCASE LETTERS
trace and repeat

N   N   N   N   N
N   N   N   N   N
N   N   N   N   N
N   N   N   N   N
N   N   N   N   N

UPERCASE LETTERS

trace and repeat

O O O O O
O O O O O
O O O O O
O O O O O
O O O O O

UPERCASE LETTERS
trace and repeat

P P P P P
P P P P P
P P P P P
P P P P P
P P P P P

UPERCASE LETTERS
trace and repeat

Q

UPERCASE LETTERS
trace and repeat

R R R R R

UPERCASE LETTERS
trace and repeat

S

UPERCASE LETTERS
trace and repeat

𝒥   𝒥   𝒥   𝒥   𝒥

UPERCASE LETTERS
trace and repeat

U

UPERCASE LETTERS
trace and repeat

V V V V V

V V V V V

V V V V V

V V V V V

V V V V V

UPERCASE LETTERS
trace and repeat

W

UPERCASE LETTERS
trace and repeat

X X X X X

UPERCASE LETTERS
trace and repeat

Y   Y   Y   Y   Y

Y   Y   Y   Y   Y

Y   Y   Y   Y   Y

Y   Y   Y   Y   Y

Y   Y   Y   Y   Y

UPERCASE LETTERS
trace and repeat

Z

lowercase letters
trace and repeat

a	*a*	*a*	*a*	*a*

lowercase letters
trace and repeat

b

lowercase letters
trace and repeat

c

lowercase letters
trace and repeat

d

lowercase letters
trace and repeat

e

lowercase letters
trace and repeat

f   f   f   f   f

f   f   f   f   f

f   f   f   f   f

f   f   f   f   f

f   f   f   f   f

lowercase letters

trace and repeat

g

lowercase letters
trace and repeat

lowercase letters
trace and repeat

i

lowercase letters
trace and repeat

lowercase letters

trace and repeat

k

lowercase letters
trace and repeat

lowercase letters
trace and repeat

m

lowercase letters
trace and repeat

n n n n n

n n n n n

n n n n n

n n n n n

n n n n n

lowercase letters
trace and repeat

o

lowercase letters
trace and repeat

p

lowercase letters
trace and repeat

q

lowercase letters
trace and repeat

r　　r　　r　　r　　r

r　　r　　r　　r　　r

r　　r　　r　　r　　r

r　　r　　r　　r　　r

r　　r　　r　　r　　r

lowercase letters
trace and repeat

s

lowercase letters
trace and repeat

t

lowercase letters
trace and repeat

u

lowercase letters
trace and repeat

v

lowercase letters
trace and repeat

w

lowercase letters
trace and repeat

x   x   x   x   x

x   x   x   x   x

x   x   x   x   x

x   x   x   x   x

x   x   x   x   x

lowercase letters
trace and repeat

y

lowercase letters
trace and repeat

z z z z z

Numbers
trace and repeat

One   One   One   One   One

One

Two   Two   Two   Two   Two

Two

Three   Three   Three   Three

Three

Four   Four   Four   Four

Four

Numbers

trace and repeat

Five Five Five Five

Five

Six Six Six Six Six

Six

Seven Seven Seven Seven

Seven

Eight Eight Eight Eight

Eight

Numbers
trace and repeat

Nine   Nine   Nine   Nine

Nine

1   1   1   1   1

2   2   2   2   2

3   3   3   3   3

4   4   4   4   4

5   5   5   5   5

6   6   6   6   6

Numbers
trace and repeat

7   7   7   7   7

8   8   8   8   8

9   9   9   9   9

!   !   !   !   !

?   ?   ?   ?   ?

@   @   @   @   @

Names of the Fruits
trace and repeat

Apple *Apple*

Banana *Banana*

Orange *Orange*

Grape *Grape*

Mango *Mango*

Plum *Plum*

Kiwi *Kiwi*

Pear *Pear*

Peach *Peach*

Names of the Vegetables
trace and repeat

Carrot   Carrot   Carrot

Onion   Onion   Onion

Potato   Potato   Potato

Beans   Beans   Beans

Corn   Corn   Corn

Tomato   Tomato   Tomato

Peas   Peas   Peas

Radish   Radish   Radish

Beet   Beet   Beet

Names of the Colors
trace and repeat

Red   *Red*

Yellow   *Yellow*

Orange   *Orange*

Pink   *Pink*

Blue   *Blue*

Purple   *Purple*

Black   *Black*

Green   *Green*

Brown   *Brown*

Names of the Animals
trace and repeat

Dog

Lion

Ostrich

Duck

Cat

Owl

Panda

Horse

Mouse

Names of the DAYS
trace and repeat

Monday *Monday*

Tuesday *Tuesday*

Wednesday *Wednesday*

Thursday *Thursday*

Friday *Friday*

Saturday *Saturday*

Sunday *Sunday*

Names of the Bodyparts
trace and repeat

Head   Head   Head

Eyes   Eyes   Eyes

Mouth   Mouth   Mouth

Shoulder   Shoulder

Chest   Chest   Chest

Elbow   Elbow

Hand   Hand   Hand

Finger   Finger   Finger

Knee   Knee   Knee

Names of the Months
trace and repeat

January *January*

February *February*

March *March*

April *April*

May *May*

June *June*

July *July*

August *August*

Names of the Months
trace and repeat

September September

October October

November November

December December

January February March

April May June

July August September

October November December

Cursive Letter writing practice
trace and repeat

Grow every day, no excuses.

Believe in your inner strength.

Challenges are hidden opportunities.

Always push your boundaries.

Cursive Letter writing practice
trace and repeat

Dreams require active pursuit.

Make today utterly amazing.

Positivity and hard work win.

limits exist to be broken.

Cursive Letter writing practice
trace and repeat

Emit positivity, attract positivity.

Start now, make it happen.

Success is a continuous journey.

Embrace new learning experiences.

Cursive Letter writing practice
trace and repeat

Yesterday's you is your benchmark.

Failure is a learning step.

Every small step counts greatly.

Lead a positively vibrant life.

Cursive Letter writing practice
trace and repeat

Improve yourself, day by day.

Potential is yours to discover.

Be someone's reason to smile.

Hope is a powerful force.

Cursive Letter writing practice
trace and repeat

Authenticity is your superpower.

Dream big, work hard.

Patience yields its own rewards.

Gratitude transforms your outlook.

Cursive Letter writing practice
trace and repeat

Mindfulness brings inner peace.

Cherish every single day.

Believe in yourself.

You light up the room.

Cursive Letter writing practice
trace and repeat

Embrace your unique sparkle.

Joy blooms from within you.

Happiness suits you beautifully.

Kindness looks amazing on you.

Cursive Letter writing practice
trace and repeat

You're doing wonderfully well.

Your laughter is contagious.

You're a breath of fresh air.

Keep being your awesome self.

Cursive Letter writing practice
trace and repeat

Coffee spills, laughter follows.

Socks mismatched, spirits matched.

Rainy days make for sunny tomorrows.

Life's a dance, you lead.

Cursive Letter writing practice
trace and repeat

Tea sips bring warm grins

Cookies burnt, memories perfectly made.

Stars can't shine without darkness.

Storms pass, rainbows await. Keep going!

Your practice

Your practice

Your practice

Your practice

Your practice

Your practice

Your practice

As your pen lifts from the paper, take a moment to acknowledge the progress you've made today. Each line drawn, every character shaped, brings you closer to the mastery of this elegant art form. Calligraphy is a journey of continuous learning and joy in each movement. So as you cap your pen, do so with the satisfaction of time well spent, knowing that with every session, your craft grows stronger.

Cherish the stillness after you've finished, the quiet pride in the marks that you've left behind. They are not just ink on paper, but a testament to your dedication and love for the art. Let this be a tranquil conclusion to your practice, and may the peace it brings stay with you until you write again.

Until next time, let the memory of the flowing ink inspire you, and remember: every word you inscribe is a reflection of your unique voice. Farewell for now, and may your calligraphy journey be as rewarding as the beautiful art you create.

www.ingramcontent.com/pod-product-compliance
Lightning Source LLC
LaVergne TN
LVHW060723020325
804889LV00012B/1223